Selections From THE WIZARD OF OZ

FLUTE

MW00575214

Editor: CAROL CUELLAR

The Wicked Witch Appears And Warns Them Not To Help Dor

FLUTE

CONTENTS

OVER THE RAINBOW

Words by
E. Y. HARBURG

Music by
HAROLD ARLEN

DING-DONG! THE WITCH IS DEAD

Lyric by
E.Y. HARBURG

Music by
HAROLD ARLEN

Ding-Dong! The Witch Is Dead - 2 - 1
IF9526

IF I ONLY HAD A BRAIN
(If I Only Had a Heart)
(If I Only Had the Nerve)

Lyric by
E.Y. HARBURG

Music by
HAROLD ARLEN

IF9526

IF I WERE KING OF THE FOREST

Lyric by
E.Y. HARBURG

Music by
HAROLD ARLEN

IF9526

LULLABY LEAGUE AND LOLLIPOP GUILD

Lyric by
E.Y. HARBURG

Music by
HAROLD ARLEN

IF9526

THE MERRY OLD LAND OF OZ

Lyric by
E.Y. HARBURG

Music by
HAROLD ARLEN

IF9526

MUNCHKINLAND

Lyric by
E.Y. HARBURG

Music by
HAROLD ARLEN

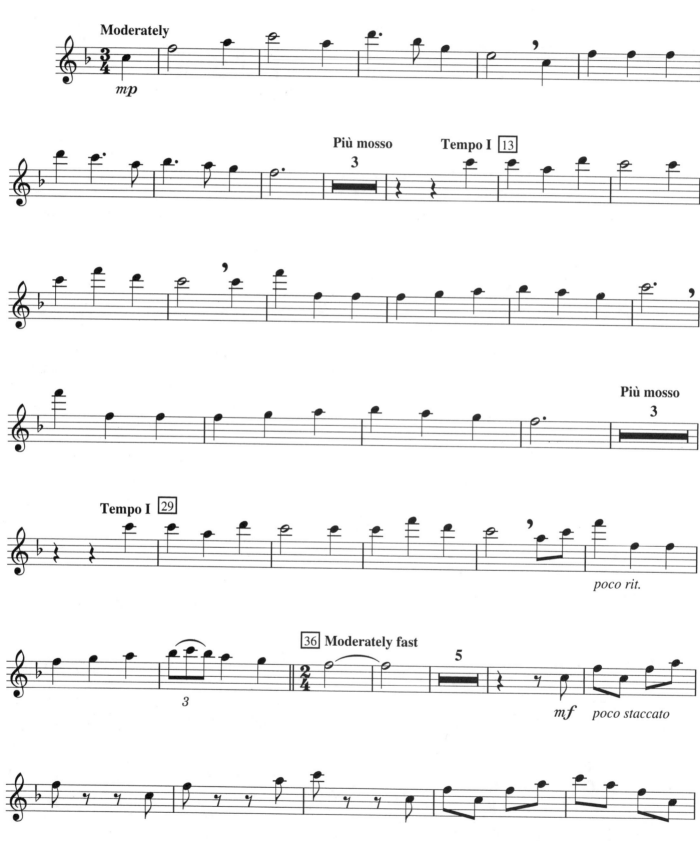

Munchkinland - 2 - 1
IF9526

legato

poco staccato

rit.

WE'RE OFF TO SEE THE WIZARD
(The Wonderful Wizard of Oz)

Lyric by
E.Y. HARBURG

Music by
HAROLD ARLEN

Moderate march tempo

We're Off to See the Wizard - 2 - 1
IF9526

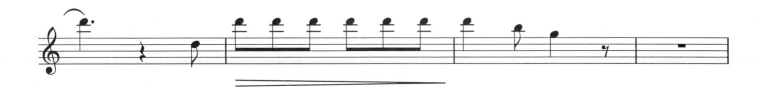

OPTIMISTIC VOICES

Lyric by
E.Y. HARBURG

Music by
HAROLD ARLEN

IF9526